75
FSG

ALSO BY HENRI COLE

Orphic Paris (2018)

Nothing to Declare (2015)

Touch (2011)

Pierce the Skin: Selected Poems (2010)

Blackbird and Wolf (2007)

Middle Earth (2003)

The Visible Man (1998)

The Look of Things (1995)

The Zoo Wheel of Knowledge (1989)

The Marble Queen (1986)

BLIZZARD

FARRAR STRAUS GIROUX

NEW YORK

HENRI COLE

Farrar, Straus and Giroux
120 Broadway, New York 10271

Printed in the United States of America
Published in 2020 by Farrar, Straus and Giroux
First paperback edition, 2021

Grateful acknowledgment is made for permission to reprint lines from "Voices from Lemnos" from *The Cure at Troy* from *Opened Ground: Selected Poems 1966–1996* by Seamus Heaney. Copyright © 1998 by Seamus Heaney. Reprinted by permission of Farrar, Straus and Giroux.

The Library of Congress has cataloged
the hardcover edition as follows:
Names: Cole, Henri, author.
Title: Blizzard / Henri Cole.
Description: First edition. | New York : Farrar, Straus and Giroux, 2020.
Identifiers: LCCN 2020012446 | ISBN 9780374114381 (hardcover)
Subjects: LCGFT: Poetry.
Classification: LCC PS3553.O4725 B58 2020 | DDC 811/.54—dc23
LC record available at https://lccn.loc.gov/2020012446

Paperback ISBN: 978-0-374-60321-2

Designed by Crisis

Our books may be purchased in bulk for promotional, educational, or business use. Please contact your local bookseller or the Macmillan Corporate and Premium Sales Department at 1-800-221-7945, extension 5442, or by email at MacmillanSpecialMarkets@macmillan.com.

www.fsgbooks.com
www.twitter.com/fsgbooks
www.facebook.com/fsgbooks

1 3 5 7 9 10 8 6 4 2

FOR RACHEL JACOFF

SOMETIMES, A FRIEND COOKS DINNER;

OUR LIVES COMMINGLE.

CONTENTS

I

II

III

NOW DO U UNDERSTAND WHAT HEAVEN IS
IT IS THE SURROUND OF THE LIVING

—James Merrill, *The Book of Ephraim*

FACE OF THE BEE

Staggering out of a black-red peony,
where you have been hiding all morning
from the frigid air, you regard me smearing
jam on dark toast. Suddenly, I am waving
my arms to make you go away. No one
is truly the owner of his own instincts,
but controlling them—this is civilization.
I thank my mother and father for this.
After they died, there were replacements
whose force upon my life I cannot measure.
With your fuzzy black face, do you see me—
a cisgender male—metabolizing
life into language, like nectar sipped
up and regurgitated into gold?

ON PEELING POTATOES

When I peel potatoes, I put my head down,
as if I am still following orders and being loyal
to my commander. I feel a connection across
time to others putting their heads down
in fatigued thought, as if this most natural
act signified living the way I wanted to,
with the bad spots cut out, and eluding
my maker. Instead of cobwebs, tumult,
and dragons, I experience an abundance
of good things, like sunlight leaking through
tall pines in the backyard. I say to myself:
This is certainly not a grunt's knowledge—
perception of a potato as my own soul—
but a sturdy, middle-aged, free man's.

BLACK MUSHROOMS

FOR SEAMUS HEANEY

The entire fungus world is wild and unnatural.
In cottony growths on the forest floor, a few spores alight,
and, if moisture and food are available, swell and grow
into protuberances, with elongating stems and raised
caps, gills, and veils. It is not always possible to identify them—
white, black, or tan; torn, bruised, or crushed—
some with squat fruit-bodies, others lacelike. Even the luxury-
  loving
Romans savored their palatal starlight. Sometimes,
when I'm suffocating from an atmosphere of restraint
within myself, I fry them up in butter, with pepper and salt,
and forget where the hurt came from. Instead, I experience
desire creating desire, and then some milder version
of a love that is temporary and guiltless, as if twigs
and bark were giving my life back its own flavor.

LINGONBERRY JAM

What a wondrous thing to suddenly be alive
eating Natalie's lingonberry jam from Alaska,
where she picked the fruit herself with one seeing eye.
In this tumultuous world we're living in—
with the one-hour news loop—my thoughts
linger, more and more, on the darkish side
as I sit at the table with Mr. & Mrs. Spork,
who still ask me, *Are you married yet?*
But Natalie's lingonberry jam pierces right
through into some deep, essential place,
where I am my own master and no sodomy
laws exist, and where, like a snowflake,
or a bee lost amid the posies, I feel
autonomous, blissed-out, and real.

TO A SNAIL

Like flesh, or consciousness inhabited
by flesh, willful, bold, *très chic*, the skin
on your gelid body is brownish from age
and secretes viscid slime from your flat
muscular foot, like script, as if Agnes Martin
had wed Caravaggio, and then, after rainfall,
you ran away, crossing a wet road with Fiats
rushing past. Where is your partner?
Contemplating your tentacles and house,
gliding on a trace of mucus from some
dark stone to who knows where,
why do I feel happiness? It's a long game—
the whole undignified, insane attempt at living—
so I've relocated you to the woods.

TO A BAT

Pulling on
leather gloves
to pick a groggy
bat from above
the front door,

I put it
outside
in a hydrangea bush.
Where are you going now,
Mr. Bat?

Can you see
your brothers and sisters
fluttering over the treetops?
Can you see
the world is crammed,

corrupt, infuriating,
shallow, sanctimonious,
and insincere?
Thank you for afflicting
my life.

Last night, even the cockroaches
looked up—*Wat dat?*—
as you flared around,
with blind eyes and pure will,
echolocating.

Ducked under
the kitchen table,
on which four eggs
huddled in a bowl,
I heard chirping—

accept and forgive,
accept and forgive—
almost beyond human hearing,
and my heart's atria beat faster,
almost healing.

JELLY

FOR BETTY BIRD AND SUSAN THOMPSON

Rubbing the bristle brush across his backbone,
securing the bridle, riding his stretched-out body
on the dirt road to town (past the Texaco station),
and following his head through hair grass and cornflowers,
she was some kind of in-between creature,
browned from the sun. To the sightless,
at the State School for the Deaf and Blind,
knowledge came in small words—under, over,
next to, inside—but it was the clip-clop of Jelly's
hooves, his fragrant mane and muscle memory
that carried her forward, hollering, *Run, Jelly. Run!*
Then, with one soft-firm *Whoa*, he did, though she
was only six, her child-hands gripping the reins tight,
hearts thumping a testimony to the love feeling.

TO THE OVERSOUL

Halfway down the grassy path,
a cemetery cat, a horse chestnut,
a concrete angel. "This is my friend,"
I wrote on blue-lined paper. "Please take
care of her. The tumor-board didn't help her.
Why did they treat her like that? She has
no mother or father. What others call *off-*
spring, these were her talismanic poems.
It doesn't take a lot of strength to hang on.
It takes strength to let go. Please tell that
to the Oversoul." Then the mommy
cat humped my leg, meowing: *Bliss,*
loss, trembling, compulsion, desire,
& disease are coffin liquor now.

THE PARTY TENT

The tent men arrived bearing sledgehammers
and were young enough to be my sons.
After rolling out the canvas, they drove rods
into the earth, heaving and grunting, with blow after blow.
When they raised the center pole, the tent went up,
with tightening ropes, and I felt my heart accelerate,
my heart that is nothing but a specialized nerve,
which my mind feeds off.

Someday, nature's undertakers—
beetles, maggots, and bottle flies—will carry it
toward the sun. Tomorrow, after the tent is gone,
a crew will remove the damaged sod,
aerate what's underneath, and apply a topdressing
of new sandy soil. Like musical notes or forms
of rock, everything will be forgotten.

AT THE GRAVE OF ROBERT LOWELL

On this tenth day of the year, I play Stravinsky
and sip vodka from a paper cup, taking in the view.
Tendrils twining, leaves rippling, guts absorbing nutrients,
brains marked by experience—all of it is dust now.
He, she, all of them lie under sod, men and women
no longer rivals in love. Bodies grow old and fester.
History is like an Impressionist painting, a variegated
landscape of emotional colors. As night falls,
owls, bats, and hedgehogs come out to hunt.
I take joy in considering my generation. I rewrite
to be read, though I feel shame acknowledging it.
Scattered among imposing trees, the ancient
and the modern intersect, spreading germs of pain
and happiness. I curl up in my fleece and drink.

RECYCLING

When the environment deteriorates,
we do, too, so I compost coffee grounds
and recycle green glass. The cadaver goes
to a friend's maggot farm where it is turned
into chicken feed. Where there is danger,
there also grows something to save us.
Bathers at the lake act upon their urges
and create an atmosphere of freedom. The thieving
financier becomes a priest with a shelter.
Me—I have no biological function and grow
like a cabbage without making divisions
of myself. Still, I have such a precise feeling
of the weeks recycling, of a stranger's arrival,
and the tumult righting itself.

DEPARTURE

During the minutes when a truck
sprays frost off the small plane's wings,

two deer graze beyond the tarmac barrier,
their limbs flexible, their rib cages pumping air.

The buck's head is adorned with a forest
that renews itself each year.

We came down from the mountain
for a ramble, the doe announces,

wearing an ice frock, sniffing his coarse hair,
the bottoms of their hooves listening to the frozen landscape.

She seems to be only partially certain
he cares for her as she cares for him.

Turning their elegance toward the runway,
they face me as I face them,

then the plane taxis onward and mounts gray
bulbous clouds in a slow dissolve.

Opening a newspaper, I can feel the altitude
against my face, but something deeper:

What was that back there? Time is short.
If tenderness approaches, run to it.

PARIS IS MY SEROQUEL

Long may I savor your organ meats
and stinky cheeses, endure your pompous
manners, breathe your gentle gardens,
wake up—beyond boredom and daydream—
under your gray skies, smiling politely
at so many dull faces passing me by,
I, who am normally so restrictive,
except in relation to him I once loved
(worn and dangerous now), each day,
kneeling down as some strange energy
penetrates my forehead, I, striving to draw
nearer to you, and to your stones, without nervousness
or regret, as all the beauty of the world
seems to touch my haunches and hooves.

HUMAN HIGHWAY

We were encountering turbulence.
I stood on a gilded balcony,
beyond which a parade of humans marched—
vagrants, self-haters, hermits, junkies,
chumps, the defeated, the paranoid,
the penniless, and those led astray by desire—
moving backwards instead of forwards,
because this is how life can be understood.
Earth fell silent, except for the gnashing teeth
of its tormentors, and it was as if we were in some kind
of holding pattern. Shadows vanished,
but daylight seemed delayed.
                                        Then, suddenly,
in the kitchen, coffee percolated.
A pussycat purred at my feet.
I cut open the throat of a grapefruit.
In the backyard, a groggy bat searched for home.
A sapling listed back and forth.
Out on the human highway,

summer rains came early to our small house
across from a cornfield,
and bread and education, too,
as happiness unfolded like a strange
psychedelic moth, or the oldest unplayable
instrument, made from a warrior's skull,
our happiness a little bone flute.

History says, Don't hope

On this side of the grave,

But then, once in a lifetime

The longed-for tidal wave

Of justice can rise up

And hope and history rhyme.

—Seamus Heaney, from *The Cure at Troy: A Version of Sophocles' "Philoctetes"*

DOVES

Gray and white, as if with age, or some preserving
of the past, as in Beowulf, our hoary ancestor,
hoary as in a bat or a willow, or the venerable
hoary dove that flew straight into my picture
window today and then lay dead on the front porch.
We buried it—in some distorted version of its normal self—
folded in a white cloth napkin in the backyard.
Still soft enough to be cut into like a cabbage, I thought,
I'm glad I'm not dead. Listen to them now,
higher up in the trees, biting and scratching,
with their unmistakable twitch of life. *Don't fear
nothing*, their twittering voices cry. The true spirit
of living isn't eating greedily, or reflection, or
even love, but dissidence, like an ax of stone.

GOYA

Three corpses bound to a tree stump,
castrated, one without arms, its head impaled
on a branch. A dark impression, richly inked,
with a delicate burnishing of figures. Pondering it,
I feel like a worm worming. If I want the truth,
I must seek it out. The line between the inner
and outer erodes, and I become a hunter putting
my face down somewhere on a path between
two ways of being—one kindly and soft;
the other an executioner. Later, out in the plaza,
I light a cigarette and have a long pull,
with small exhales, taking the measure
of my own hand, its lustrous hairy
knuckles dinged from grinding meat.

WEEPING CHERRY

On a plateau, with little volcanic mountains,
a muddy river, dangerous when the snow melts,
a fertile valley, cattle breeders, and a music academy,
a tall, handsome, agile people, with straight black hair
and an enterprising spirit, lived peaceably. Though
there had never been hatred between the races,
after a quarrel over local matters, massacres came.
Men, women, and children robbed and deported—
an evacuation, they called it. Heads impaled on branches.
Mounds of corpses, like grim flowers knotted together.
A passing ship transported a few to a distant port,
where Mother was born, though now she, too,
has vanished into the universe, and the cold browns
the weeping cherry, vivid red mixed with blue.

MIGRANTS DEVOURING THE FLESH OF A DEAD HORSE

Since there's no time for grinding or cooking,
it's best not to drag the parts too far.
As the solitary knife goes in and out,
the mama is exhausted but also rather mild
in her expression, and the baby resembles
a seahorse compelled to know something painful.
No one appears left out—stabbing, licking, or chewing—
or sees the texture of the animal's insides
mirrored in the fluttering of cloth, not lightness
or delicacy, but something more basic,
related to the moist earth. Once this horse ornamented
a field, with its flexible limbs and nuzzling head.
Eat me, it neighs now. The tree of life
is greater than all the helicopters of death.

TO A ROOT IN AIR

Swatting flies from their faces, the boys
play in garbage heaps of burned corncobs
and crushed plastic bottles. Their tear-rimmed
eyes do not seem to bother them. Men chop wood
for fires in tin drums, as if part of some precarious
covenant camped out in shipping containers
on a wind-beaten plain. After turning to smugglers
for passage, they try to seize some knowledge
of good, a second act of sorts, in which their wives
may conceive and their sons not unman them.
Look, there in the white sunlight, a tea rose
is blooming, dug up from a garden far away,
still vivid pink from a woman's energy,
with a hirsute root in air.

(RE)CREATION

Preferring the company of nature to man,
disappointed in love, he retreated to the desert.
But this was not any ordinary desert,
for helicopters and jets appeared overhead. A parade of camels.
When a lion came out of the darkness,
the man was angry at his horse for not warning him.
Far away, it was difficult to see the minarets in a steep-sided valley.
When the Taliban seized him,
they put a noose around his neck,
and he messed his pants.
Far away, a flute played, a missile launched,
and a child kneeled drinking before a well.
Still, whatever the faults of life,
the merriment of it was only partially erased
by the curious flies of Allah investigating
the carrion hanging in the public square.
It was as if this had not once been a man at all,
but instead a white-winged dove,
its solitary neck and breast washed lightly with pink.

Flocks of these doves are a common sight in summer,
nesting in fragile platforms of twigs,
eating small seeds from the desert willow.
On takeoff, they produce, with their wings,
a subtle, unearthly whistle.

SUPER BLOOM

America, like a monstrous sow
vomiting cars and appliances into a green ooze
of dollar bills, where is my America?
Agnostic and uninsured, I eat celery, onions,
and garlic—my Holy Trinity of survival. I go
to the desert and celebrate death-life, picking a nosegay
for my room at the Motel 6. You said you would always
tell the truth, Mr. President, but that was a lie, so I'm
pressing my white face to your White House door,
a kind of pig keeper with an urge for happiness.
At the Morbidity Conference, they said we can't know
our own strength. They said we're like roses sprayed
with pesticide. They said one man in a long black car
can't ever really empty out the fullness.

GROSS NATIONAL UNHAPPINESS

No, I am not afraid of you
descending the long white marble steps
from a White Hawk helicopter
to a state-sponsored spectacle
of mansplaining and lies.
If you divide the sea,
you will wind up in a ditch.
The she-goat will mount the he-goat.
Good deeds will cut out our tongues.
No tree will penetrate a radiant sky.
Can't you see our tents cannot be separated?
Can't you see your one thousand dogs
are not greater than our
one thousand gazelles?

UNSTABLE AIR

I was looking
for the two
black men,
who'd fought
in the Revolutionary War,

buried under
slate slabs
carved with curly-
haired cherubs.
Most of the tablets

had no names
and were broken.
Schoolboys
played ball
on the little mounds

that still looked fresh.
The sun was hard white,
and a chestnut tree
shaded my eyes.
A dense, ball-shaped,

branchy shrub,
with lacy florets,
seemed to represent
the puzzlement of dying
in order to live,

or the paradox
of lying in the tomb
of one's master,
whose dust was
as white as yours.

MUD OR FLESH

Before he enters his cell, he strips
and hears a voice muttering,
Well, look how far you've come.
A shy, gruff person, he thinks,
I'm just killing time now.

Though at first he lives and breathes in the mode
of *himself*, soon he forgets the taste of his own lips.
He is just number 15,
on the 11th block, pressing his ear to the vent,
getting up on the gate to listen to fighting,
eating, moaning, and laboring.

I got to have my radio.
I got to keep my mouth shut,
my teeth unexposed.
I got to sleep sitting up.

Every morning, he has his *me* time
on the rusty bowl, at the steel sink, on the saggy mattress.
Gazing at smeared sky,
through a parapet hole above the catwalk,
he forgets the perdition of souls.
He is only a man who once loved number 46
(from the commissary), then number 73
(scrounging cigarettes), then number 44
(fair enough).

Scrubbing off the past that cannot be scrubbed off,
someone leaves the water running,
and Justice comes running with a clinking coil of keys.
No bare feet in the shower. Sleep, eat, shit
when they tell you. Touching only at the start
and end of visitor hour.

A fly dancing around his head believes
he is meat in a refrigerator locker, a fly
that doesn't mind bare walls and recites
for the benefit of his senses:
"Am not I /
A fly like thee?"

Each hour takes small, slow steps, like a drummer
at a funeral. Doing push-ups, he mourns
the moments, like gondolas
dangling from a cable, that created him.
Am I mud or flesh?
                                        Lying alone
under bright lamp lights, he hears, far off,
the sounds of the city still beckoning
and feels the airways in his chest tightening,
as his soul-animal huddles with others
in some final agglomeration.

HAIKU

After the sewage flowed into the sea
and took the oxygen away, the fishes fled,
but the jellies didn't mind. They stayed
and ate up the food the fishes left behind.
I sat on the beach in my red pajamas
and listened to the sparkling foam,
like feelings being fustigated. Nearby,
a crayfish tugged on a string. In the distance,
a man waved. Unnatural cycles seemed to be
establishing themselves, without regard to our lives.
Deep inside, I could feel a needle skip:

Autumn dark.
Murmur of the saw.
Poor humans.

THE HORSEMEN

After the flag juggling and the reading of a challenge,
two horsemen charged the effigy of a Saracen—
striking his shield with their lances. He, then,
rotated, threatening the horsemen with his heavy
whip armed with lead and leather balls.
The horseman disarmed lost all his points.
The horseman struck by the whip lost two points.
The horseman hitting the Saracen won
a double score. Then all the knights, soldiers,
musicians, valets, jugglers, and jousters assembled
for the presentation of the golden lance,
but none seemed immortal or free. So I lay in some
violets for a while and luxuriated in the sun,
until shadow swallowed up the street.

PHEASANT

After espresso, friendly banter, and cold
meats; after the shots taken, the near misses,
and more shots; after frenzy in thick woods,
barking pointers, and sprays of grapeshot;
after the trembling, hollering, and retrieving;
after a long table of antipasti, slow-cooked beans,
and tarts served alongside fruit—the pheasant
lay gutted or hung up for moist roasting.
Preferring to run rather than fly, timid around men,
how they startled upward with a wing-whir.
Now I eat what is caught with my own hands
like my father, and feel confused. The charm
flees. I want my life to be borrowing and
paying back. I don't want to be a gun.

LAND OF NEVER-ENDING HOLES

I don't want you to leave.

I don't want you to leave this place I so love, where
underbrush, jackrabbits,
and the desert press in on us.

Waiting under a date palm, with a suitcase and cell phone,
listening for the train whistle—this is how I picture you.

Don't strut or you will stumble.

Make your mess into a message.

Make your roof tight and your clothing sufficient,
and you shall never be wanting if you value "the best
property of all—
friends" (Emerson).

Remember the Zen axiom: Nothing lasts, nothing is finished,
and nothing is perfect.

Out there is a land of never-ending holes, where brown is the
new green.

Out there are omnivorous, dazzling human voices—coarse
cries, airy falsettos, heady
blues, soul, and solemn low rumbles—speaking and
teaching.

It is never useless to say something or teach someone.

The obscure human soul—it is sad and happy at once.

Men sweep and stir up the dust, but women sprinkle water and
settle it,
sweetening the air.

Out there, it is swarming, venal, frivolous, vexing, crude, and
hypocritical,
but you must never cease to listen, look, and feel.

If you love a zebra, do not settle for a tapir.

Think of all you have so far as a shelter made of tarp and rope,
and build
something marvelous.

Uplift, transformation, radiance—when you turn the old horse
toward them,
he will always pick up his step.

See those bulbous clouds forming over the small San Gabriel
Mountains?

They are greater than any tanks or armored vehicles.

See out there beyond the ash, avocado, lemon, and peppertrees,
a little trail ends at a highway leading to spin rooms and
war rooms,
but also there are bee spawn, motion dazzle, and
maple syrup.

I don't want you to leave.

Out there, in the land of never-ending holes,
may those who love you love you, as in the proverb,
but may God turn the hearts of those who cannot love you,
and if he cannot turn their hearts, may he turn their ankles,
so you will know them by their limping.

In 1986 when the Court ruled in *Bowers v. Hardwick* that the constitutional right of privacy does not extend to homosexual behavior, Justice Blackmun wrote in dissent:

> *The fact that individuals define themselves in a significant way through their intimate sexual relationships with others suggests, in a Nation as diverse as ours, that there may be many "right" ways of conducting those relationships, and that much of the richness of a relationship will come from the freedom an individual has to choose the form and nature of these intensely personal bonds.*

ON PRIDE

I lived in a rooming house then
and tried to be good but was a real
disappointment. A man without cunning
is like an empty matchbox. I can't remember
now the sad, slow procession of words
between us. Only the hurt. *Plug the hole*
if the patient is bleeding, I thought.
If you do the right thing in the first three minutes
you'll survive. So we put ice cubes on our napes.
My pride was like a giant, oblong
pumpkin. My words were farting on stone.
Then I kissed you until your face became red.
I can't remember now where the words flew off to,
but what an awful hurt.

(*after Apollinaire*)

RED DAWN

The transfer is done in a dark room
with a red light to keep them calm.

Still, it's stressful, hanging upside down,
when an electrical pulse shuts their hearts down,
and the plucking rubber fingers
and mechanical-rotary knife begin,
the shackle line continually moving,
like sterile meditations on a life,
or the sacrifices one makes for an enigmatic love.

As their legs, thighs, and wings are removed,
their heads are pulled off in a channel,
their hearts and livers preserved as edible offal.

Even in death, will I still want you?
Don't want, can have. Can't have, want.
Sometimes, the empty languor
of the present is almost unbearable.
Worms, crickets, minnows—
after the night, how do they recover so fully?

ELEVATION

Pigs eat the rats that eat the corn,
and we eat the pigs and forget about this.
Life cannot shake off death.
                                        Like a study in genteelness,
you were neatly dressed in a jacket
and trousers. Removing your coffin,
they leant it up against a wall. Things always
start out organized and get messier.
Outside, birds scattered, *jip-jip* and *pip-pip-pip*,
as some new version of America became itself.

Each night I dreamed the dream called *elevation*
in which a wondrous man sought my hand and my heart.
Then I awoke, and he departed.
                                        Look at the flock of pigeons
flying into a thunderhead! I always feel an elevation
when small things overmaster the great.

KEEP ME

I found a necktie on the street, a handmade
silk tie from an Italian designer. *Keep me,*
it pleaded from the trash. There's probably
a story it could tell me of calamity days long ago.
Then yesterday, tying a Windsor knot around
my neck, I heard voices, *Why have you got*
that old tie on? Suddenly, Mason, Roy, Jimmy,
and Miguel were pulling at my arms, like it was
the '80s again, a darksome decade, with another
hard-right president. My lips were not yet content
with stillness. We were on our way home
from a nightclub. *I adore you,* Miguel moaned,
but have to return now. Remember
death ends a life, not a relationship.

EPIVIR, D4T, CRIXIVAN

The new disease came, but not without warning.
The drugs were a toxic combo that kept the sick going
another year. I loved how you talked in your sleep
about free will. Your clothes smelled, but the blood
levels were normal. *Now I have seen the sun god*:
this is what I thought when I first saw you—the face,
the bearing—but perfection of form meant nothing
to you, and we were all just souls carrying around
a corpse. I smoked cannabis while the government slept.
Drug companies held parties in Arizona and Florida.
The profit motive always thrives. To those who didn't
sell well in the bars, it felt like Revenge of the Nerds.
Goaded by your hand, I wrote poems, an essence
squeezed out of this matter, memory now.

GINGER AND SORROW

My skin is the cover of my body.
It keeps me bound to my surroundings.
It is the leather over my spine.
It is the silk over the corneas of my eyes.
Where I am hairless, at the lips and groin,
there is pinkness and vulnerability.
Despite a protective covering of horny skin,
there is no such problem with my fingers,
whose ridges and grooves are so gratifying
to both the lover and the criminologist.
I think perhaps the entire history
of me is here—viper of memory,
stab of regret, red light of oblivion.
Hell would be living without them.

RICE PUDDING

Hansel and Gretel were picking strawberries
and listening to a bronze cuckoo.
As the forest mist thickened,
Hansel snuggled up to his little sister,
admitting they were lost.
They were the children
of a broom maker who drank too much.
They did not understand that a wife
is to a husband what the husband makes her,
or that even in our misery life goes on.
Squirrels play. Bees forage. Hemlocks bow.

Sitting at the kitchen table, I eat yesterday's meat,
peas and carrots, with a bowl of rice pudding.
Now that you are dead, my stubborn heart lives.

BLIZZARD

As soon as I am doing nothing,
I am not able to do anything,
existing quietly behind lock and key,
like a cobweb's mesh.
It's 4 a.m.
The voices of birds do not multiply into a force.
The sun does not engross from the East.
A fly roams the fingers on my right hand
like worms. Somewhere, in an empty room, a phone rings.
On the street, a bare tree shadows a brownstone.
(Be precise about objects, but reticent about feelings,
the master urged.)
I need everything within
to be livelier. Infatuation, sadism, lust: I remember them,

but memory of feeling is not feeling,
a parasite is not the meat it lived on.

DANDELIONS (III)

Everyone has secrets—moments that change them.
I tell my secrets to some dandelions hugging the lichen-like turf.
He was doing lines on a mirror and had sugar spots on his nose.
It made him seem focused, with a conversational prowess.
I was in some kind of low-oxygen dead zone. You flee or suffocate.
Only jellies survive. Maybe I was afraid of emptiness—*horror vacui.*
After the insufflation of the only real love of his life, he texted a
    stranger.
I was brooding. *You will never disembarrass yourself from this.*
Then my love-hate carried me home. *There, I'm done with it*,
I thought, full of my own idea, like transparent glass
made less invisible by a light that goes straight through it
and then bends into a spectrum. Or like a winter day,
when a low bluish sunlight memorializes everything
and long shadows darken out to a void.

ON FRIENDSHIP

Lately, remembering anything involves an ability
to forget something else. Watching the news,
I writhe and moan; my mind is not itself.
Lying next to a begonia from which black ants come and go,
I drink a vodka. Night falls. This seems a balm
for wounds that are not visible in the gaudy daylight.
Sometimes, a friend cooks dinner; our lives commingle.
In loneliness, I fear me, but in society I'm like a soldier
kneeling on soft mats. Everything seems possible,
as when I hear birds that awaken at 4 a.m. or see
a veil upon a face. Beware the heart is lean red meat.
The mind feeds on this. I carry on my shoulder
a bow and arrow for protection. I believe whatever
I do next will surpass what I have done.

CORPSE POSE

Waiting for a deceased friend's cat to die
is almost unbearable. *This is where you live now,*
I explain. *Please stop crying.* But he is like a widower
in some kind of holding pattern around a difficult truth.
His head, his bearing, his movements are handsome to me,
a kind of permanent elsewhere devoted to separation and death.
Please, let's try to forget, dear. We need each other.
I feel I want to tell him something, but I'm not sure what.
So much about life doesn't make sense. Each night,
I do the corpse pose, and he ponders me, with his corpse face,
licking his coat. The Egyptians first tamed his kind.
Their dead were buried in galleries closed up with stone slabs.
When my friend and I were young,
we tramped through woods of black oaks.

MAN AND KITTEN

It is such a curiously pleasant thing to hold
the tenseness of a kitten—barefooted
and subordinate—with soft, assertive tongue.
Teaching it what I know, I think, *It loves me.*
A man is very nearly a god, a kitten nothing.
A man is self-praising, answering to nobody.
A kitten chooses slavery over hunger.
Tonight: mushrooms and bean curd,
with lemon sauce. A kitten will eat anything.
Its life is mine now. It seems to like this.
It doesn't know my phone doesn't ring.
It doesn't know it reveals my life in a new light,
even secured by a string. Suddenly, there is
trance, illumination, spectacle.

KAYAKING ON THE CHARLES

I don't really like the ferries that make the water a scary vortex,
or the blurry white sun that blinds me, or the adorable small
families
of distressed ducklings that swim in a panic when a speedboat cuts
through, spewing a miasma into the river, but I love the Longfellow
Bridge's towers that resemble the silver salt and pepper canisters
on my kitchen table. They belonged to Mother. The Department
of Transportation is restoring the bridge masonry now. Paddling
under
its big arches, I feel weary, as memory floats up, ignited by cigarette
butts thrown down by steelworkers. I want to paddle away, too.
Flies investigate my bare calves, and when I slap them hard
I realize they are so happy. I'm their amusement. Sometimes
memories involve someone I loved. A rope chafes a cleat.
I want my life to be post-pas de deux now. Lord, look at me,
hatless, with naked torso, sixtyish, paddling alone upriver.

GAY BINGO AT A PASADENA ANIMAL SHELTER

My bingo cards are empty, because I'm not paying attention.
I can't hear the numbers, because something inward is being
given substance.
Then my mother and father appear in the bingo hall and seem
sad and solitary.
They are shades now, with pale skin, and have no shame showing
their genitals.
This is before I am born and before a little strip of DNA—
mutated in the '30s and '40s, part chimpanzee—overran the
community
and before the friends of my youth are victims of discrimination.
I resemble my mother and father, but if you look closer,
you will see that I am different, I am Henri.
Don't pay no mind to the haters, Mother and Father are
repeating,
and I listen poignantly, not hearing the bingo numbers called.
I think maybe my real subject is writing as an act of revenge
against the past:
The beach was so white; O, how the sun burned;

he loved me as I loved him, but we did what others told us
and kept this hidden. Now, I make my own decisions.
I don't speak so softly. Tonight, we're raising money for the
    shelter animals.
The person I call *myself*—elegant, libidinous, austere—
is older than many buildings here, where time moves too swiftly,
taking the measure of my body, like hot sand or a hand leaving
    its mark,
and the bright sunlight blurs the days into one another.
Still, the sleeping heart awakens,
and, pricked and fed, it grows plump again.

ACKNOWLEDGMENTS

For their encouragement, I am indebted to the editors of the following publications, where poems, sometimes in different forms, were originally published:

Ambit: "To a Bat"

The American Poetry Review: "Goya" and "To a Root in Air"

The American Scholar: "Dandelions (III)," "Face of the Bee," "Gross National Unhappiness," "Keep Me," and "On Peeling Potatoes"

The Believer: "Super Bloom"

Los Angeles Review of Books: "Jelly"

The Nation: "Epivir, d4T, Crixivan," "Gay Bingo at a Pasadena Animal Shelter," and "Weeping Cherry"

The New Criterion: "The Horsemen" and "To a Snail"

The New Yorker: "Doves" and "On Friendship"

The New York Review of Books: "Black Mushrooms" and "Blizzard"

The Paris Review: "At the Grave of Robert Lowell," "Corpse Pose," "Kayaking on the Charles," "On Pride," "The Party Tent," "Red Dawn," "Rice Pudding" as "No Homecoming," and "Unstable Air"

Poetry: "Haiku"

Poetry Ireland: "(Re)creation"

Raritan: "Elevation" and "Human Highway"

Salmagundi: "Ginger and Sorrow," "Lingonberry Jam," "Man and Kitten," and "Migrants Devouring the Flesh of a Dead Horse"

The Threepenny Review: "Recycling"

The Times Literary Supplement: "Departure"

Claremont McKenna College commencement poem: "Land of Never-Ending Holes"

I Know Now in Wonder: 25 Poems from the First 25 Years of the Civitella Ranieri Foundation (Persea Books): "Pheasant"

Poems of Paris (Everyman's Library Pocket Poets Series): "Paris Is My Seroquel"

I wish to thank the Radcliffe Institute for Advanced Study at Harvard University, the Civitella Ranieri Foundation, and the Blue Mountain Center for their support and friendship.

Cover photograph by Charlie Gross.